ACTIVITY BOOK 1

T0344042

Contents

Welcome

1 Trace. Then match.

1 _Hello_ ,
I'm Rose.

2 _Hello_ ,
I'm Charlie.

3 _Hello_ ,
I'm Uncle Dan.

4 _Hello_ ,
I'm Ola.

a

b

c

d

2  Trace and colour.

1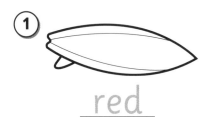
red

2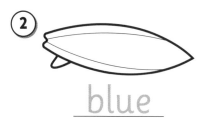
blue

3
yellow

4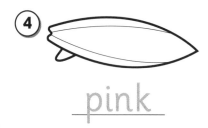
pink

5
green

6
orange

3  **Read. Then colour.**

| 1 = red | 2 = yellow | 3 = green | 4 = orange |
| 5 = blue | 6 = pink | 7 = purple |

Count with me.

4  **Trace.**

1 one   2 two   3 three   4 four   5 five

6 six   7 seven   8 eight   9 nine   10 ten

1 My toys

1 Match. Then trace and say.

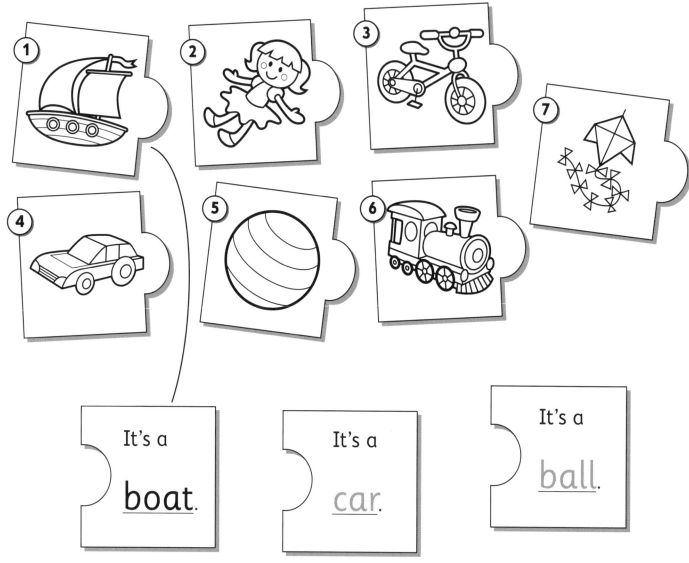

 **Listen and ✔ or ✗. Then colour.**

①  ✔

②  ☐

③  ☐

   Trace. Then draw and colour.

① It's a train.
It's **red**.

② It's a bike.
It's blue.

③ It's a ball.
It's purple.

④ It's a car.
It's green.

⑤ It's a doll.
It's yellow.

⑥ It's a kite.
It's pink.

4 Match and say.

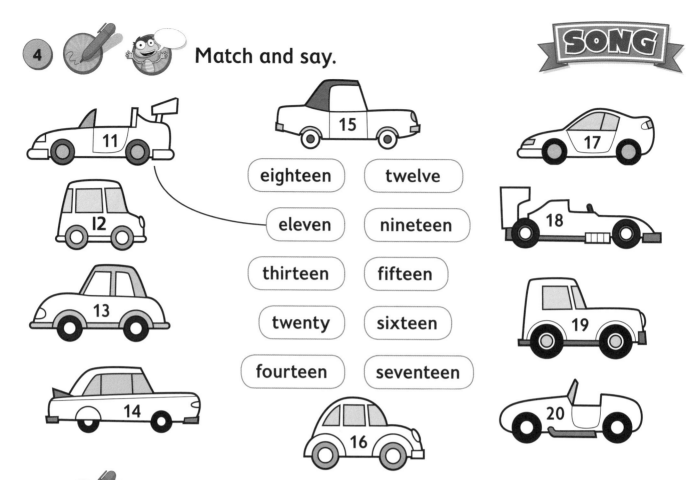

eighteen twelve

eleven nineteen

thirteen fifteen

twenty sixteen

fourteen seventeen

5 Find and count. Then write.

Start

Finish

TOYS

How many balls? _____ balls.

6   Listen and number.
Then trace and match.

SOUNDS FUN!

frog 1

box ☐

doll ☐

pen ☐

hen ☐

ten ☐

7 Find and colour.

e = red

o = orange

Listen and colour. Then write.

~~ball~~ boat doll train

1 It's yellow.

It's a **ball**.

2 It's pink.

It's a _____.

3 It's green.

It's a _____.

4 It's blue.

It's a _____.

9  **Read and colour. Then write.**

It's a kite.

It's _____.

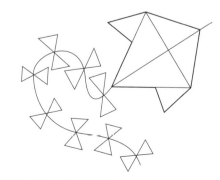

 10  **Listen and write.**

1    = __4__ dolls

2     = _____ trains

3   = _____ bike

4    = _____ boats

11  **Write. Then say.**

1   __11__

2 ✚   _____

3 ━   _____

 **Read and colour. Then circle.**

1 It's blue. It's a (car / ball).

2 It's green. It's a (doll / bike).

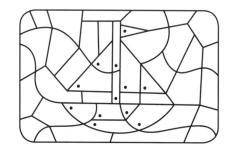

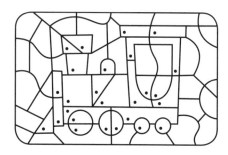

3 It's yellow. It's a (kite / boat).

4 It's purple. It's a (doll / train).

 **Read and colour.**

It's a car. It's red.

Ten dolls.

It's a train.

It's blue.

2 My family

1 Read and match. Then say.

This is my family.

aunt | uncle | granny

cousin | grandad | friend

Read and circle.

1. (He's / (She's)) my friend.

2. (He's / She's) my cousin.

3. (He's / She's) my grandad.

4. (He's / She's) my uncle.

5. (He's / She's) my sister.

6. (He's / She's) my granny.

3 **Listen and match.**

① mum

② dad

③ sister

④ granny

⑤ grandad

Where's my...?

4  **Now circle and write. Then say.**

~~bedroom~~   kitchen   living room

1   Where's my sister?   (He's /(She's)) in the _____bedroom_____ .

2   Where's my granny?   (He's / She's) in the _____ .

3   Where's my grandad?   (He's / She's) in the _____ .

5 Listen and match. Then trace.

SOUNDS FUN!

1

2

3

4

5

mum   dad

bus   van

bug   map

6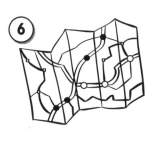

  6 Listen and circle the odd one out.

1

2

3

4

 **Look and number. Then say.**

①  ②  ③  ④

 **2**

Look! It's mum.

  Read and circle.

1 Look, it's (mum / granny). **2** Look, it's (grandad / Uncle Dan).

3 Look, it's your (aunt / mum). **4** Look, it's your (friend / grandad).

aunt ~~baby~~ brother grandad granny sister uncle

1

baby

①    ②    ③    ④

a He's young.   **b** She's young.   **c** She's old.   **d** He's old.

 **11** Read and look. Then write.

I CAN DO IT!

1 Where's my ___aunt___ ? She's in the bedroom.

2 Where's my _____? He's in the kitchen.

3 Where's my _____? She's in the living room.

4 Where's my _____? She's in the bathroom.

~~aunt~~
grandad
granny
friend

 **12** Read. Then find and ✓.

Where's my uncle?

He's in the bathroom.

LOOK!

Where's my cousin?

She's in the kitchen.

He's in the house.

3 My body

 Number and say.

1) arms 2) body 3) feet 4) fingers
5) hands 6) head 7) ~~legs~~ 8) toes

 7

 **Look and write. Then say.**

~~arms~~   body   feet   hands   legs   toes

(1) Wave your ___arms___ .

(2) Clap your _____ .

(3) Move your _____ .

(4) Shake your _____ .

(5) Stamp your _____ .

(6) Touch your _____ .

I've got three arms. I've got nine fingers.
I've got four feet and eight toes. I'm green.

 **Listen and write. Then draw.**

1 I've got _____4_____ arms.

2 I've got _____ legs.

3 I've got _____ hands.

4 I've got _____ feet.

5 I've got _____ fingers.

6 I've got _____ toes.

7 I'm _____.

SOUNDS FUN!

5 Listen and match.
Then trace.

1

2

3

feet   fish

three   sister

green   pink

4

5

6

6 Match. Then listen and check.

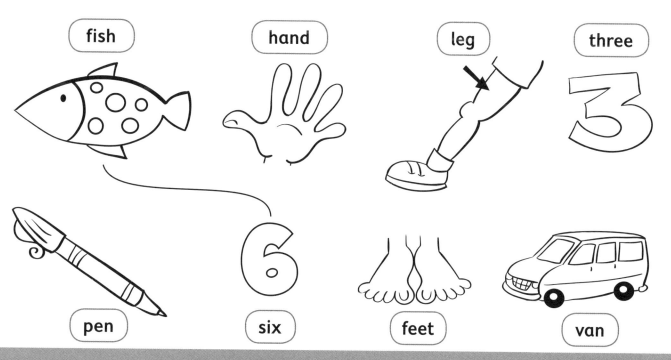

fish   hand   leg   three

pen   six   feet   van

Listen and match.

1 Jump! Touch your toes!

2 This is fun!

3 Can you help? It's the bus.

a

b

c

  Read and number.

a

2

b

1   Stand on your head.

2   Touch your toes.

3   Move your body.

4   Stand on one leg.

c

d

 **Look and write. Then say.**

dance   hop   jump

① _____   ② _____   ③ _____

 Read and find. Then number.

5 Wave your arms.

☐ Jump.

☐ Clap your hands.

☐ Touch your toes.

☐ Dance.

PE

3

 **Look and write. Then say.**

| arms | ~~body~~ | eight | hand |
| ~~one~~ | six | toes | two |

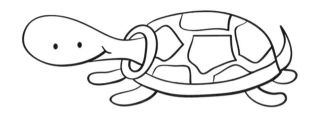

1 I've got <u>**one body**</u> .

2 I've got _____.

3 I've got _____.

4 I've got _____.

  Read and circle.

Clap your hands. /
Stamp your feet.

LOOK!

I've got ten fingers.

Clap your hands.

Wave your arms.

4 My face

1  Look and write. Then say.

ears   eyes   ~~face~~   hair   mouth   nose

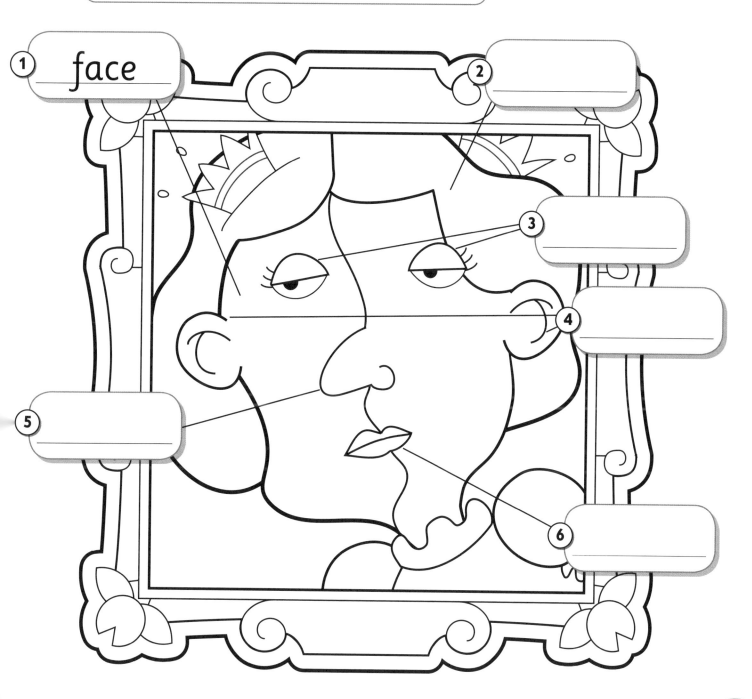

1 _face_

2 ____

3 ____

4 ____

5 ____

6 ____

2  **Read and match.**

1

2   small eyes   short hair

     big eyes   a big nose

3   long hair   a small nose

4

5

6

3 **Read. Then look and write.**

1

2

I've got big eyes.   ⬚ 2

I've got a big nose.   ⬚

I've got small eyes.   ⬚

I've got short hair.   ⬚

I've got long hair.   ⬚

I've got a big mouth.   ⬚

4   **Listen and colour.**

5   **Read. Then look and circle.**

1 She's got big eyes. ⟨Yes⟩ / No

2 He's got long hair. Yes / No

3 She's got a small mouth. Yes / No

4 He's got a small nose. Yes / No

5 She's got short hair. Yes / No

6   Listen and number.
Then trace.

clothes ☐

nose ☐

old ☐

baby ☐

play 1

shapes ☐

7   Find and colour. Then say.

o = red

a = blue

8   **Read and draw.**

He's got big eyes.
He's got short
black hair.
He's got a small
mouth.

 9   **Read and ✔ or ✘.**

1

She's got a small nose. ✔

2

He's got small eyes. ☐

3

She's got long hair. ☐

4

He's got glasses. ☐

 **10**  **Count and write. Then say.**

1

 **11** **Listen. Then look and circle.**

1 (Yes) / No   **2** Yes / No   **3** Yes / No   **4** Yes / No

 12 **Draw. Then write and say.**

It's a _____.

13  **Read. Then look and write.**

big long ~~short~~ small small

①

He's got _____short_____ hair.

She's got _____ eyes.

He's got a _____ mouth.

She's got _____ hair.

He's got _____ ears.

②

14 2:16 **Listen and number.**

   1

She's got small eyes.

LOOK!

He's got a small nose.

She's got long hair.

It's a circle.

5 Animals

1 **Look and write. Then say.**

cow   duck   ~~goat~~   hen   horse   sheep   turkey

1 goat

2

3

4

5

6

7

 **Colour. Then say.**

 1

2

3

4

 **Look at Activity 2. Then read and write _Yes_ or _No_.**

1

2

3

Is it a horse? __Yes__

Is it a cow? _____

Is it a sheep? _____

4

5

Is it a duck? _____

Is it a goat? _____

4  Look and write.

cat   duck   frog   ~~horse~~

1

2

3

4

horse _____   _____   _____

5  Read. Then look and write.

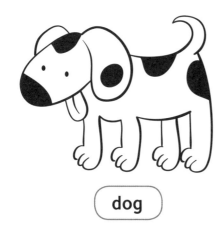

(dog)   (hen)   (sheep)

1   It's got big ears.   It's a ___dog___.

2   It's got two legs.   It's a _____.

3   It's got white legs.   It's a _____.

4   It's got a black face.   It's a _____.

6  Listen and match. Then trace.

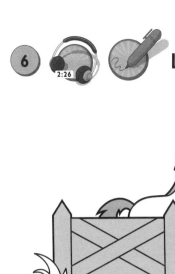

horse   cow

1 crown   2 four   3 house   4 torch

7 Listen and circle two words.

horse

1   eye / torch / arm / four

2   jump / brown / mouth / orange

cow

goat

3   nose / three / clothes / dad

4   crown / mum / bug / head

duck

8 **Look and say. Then write.**

STORY

goat ~~hen~~ horse skunk

1 It's a ___hen___ !

2 It's a _____ !

3 It's a _____ !

4 It's a _____ !

 **9** **Read and match.**

1 It's got two legs. It's small.

2 It's small. It's black and white.

3 It's big. It's black and white.

4 It's got four legs. It's grey.

a **b**

c **d**

10  Match. Then say.

1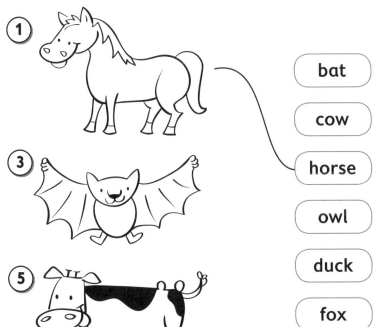

bat

cow

horse

owl

duck

fox

2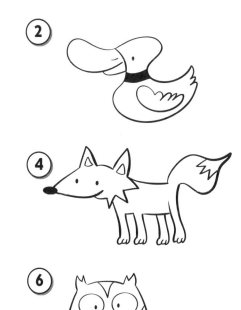

3

4

5

6

11  Draw animals from Activity 10.
Then listen and check.

day

night

Lesson 6

Where is Uncle Dan? Listen and follow the path.

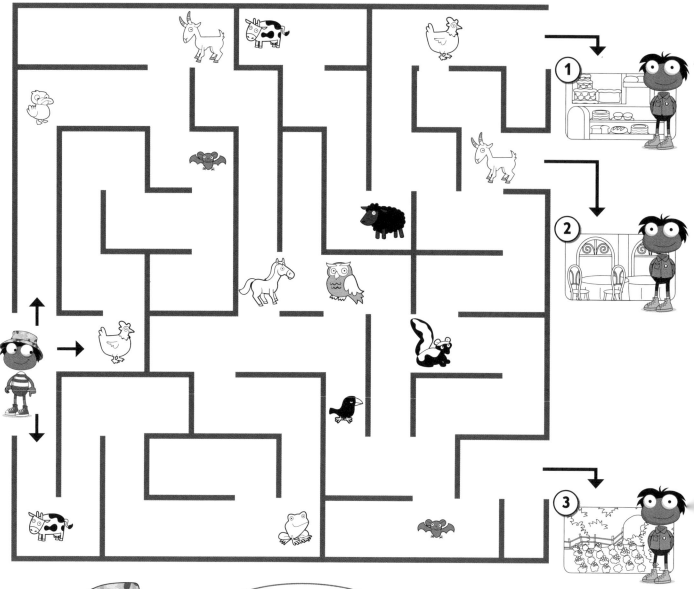

  It's got big eyes.

LOOK!

It's fat.

It's got four legs.

Is it a cow?

6 Food

1  Look and write. Then draw and say.

apples   bananas   burgers   chicken
~~eggs~~   hot dogs   pizza   rice

1 eggs
2 _____
3 _____
4 _____
5 _____
6 _____
7 _____
8 _____
9 _____

Look and write. Then say.

| apples | bananas | ~~chicken~~ | eggs |

1 I like **chicken**.

2 I like _____.

3 I like _____.

4 I like _____.

 **Read and look. Then circle and say.**

I like...

apples bananas (chicken) eggs fish hot dogs pizza rice

Listen and draw.

  **Find and write. Then say.**

1 I like _____ **fish** _____ and

2 I don't like _____ or

_____.

_____.

6 **Find and colour.**

bike   mice   rice

 SOUNDS FUN!

7 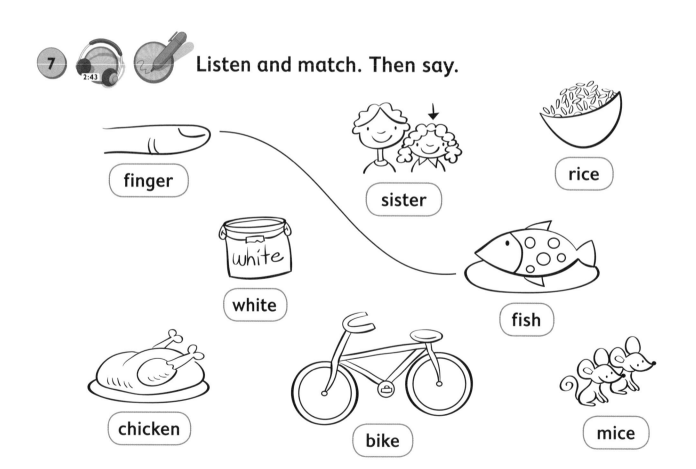 **Listen and match. Then say.**

finger

sister

rice

white

fish

chicken

bike

mice

8   **Read and draw.**

I like...

apple cake	chicken	burgers	bananas

I like...

milk	rice	banana milkshakes	apples

9 **Circle and draw.**

I like (burgers / hot dogs).

I like (fish / chicken).

 **10** **Read. Then look and number.**

1 I like toast and bananas for breakfast.

2 I like cereal for breakfast.

3 I like pizza for lunch.

4 I like fish and salad for dinner.

  1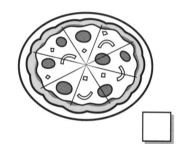

11 **Find and circle.**

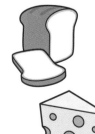

c	h	e	e	s	e	f	a	c
r	p	i	z	z	a	i	p	h
i	t	o	a	s	t	s	p	i
c	e	r	e	a	l	h	l	c
e	d	s	a	l	a	d	e	k
g	f	b	a	n	a	n	a	e
g	r	b	r	e	a	d	h	n

Listen and circle. Then write.

I like...
cereal
(chicken)
cheese
fish
apples
salad

I don't like...
toast
pizza
bread
bananas
eggs
rice

1 I like ____**chicken**____
and _____.

2 I don't like _____
or _____.

  Read and circle.

LOOK!

I like apples.

I don't like pizza.

I like toast for breakfast.

I don't like...

pizza
chicken   hot dogs   rice
(apples)   eggs
        burgers   bananas

7 Clothes

1 Find and colour. Then write.

dress   shoe   ~~skirt~~   socks   trousers   T-shirt

1 an orange ___skirt___   **2** blue _____

3 a pink _____   **4** a red _____

5 a brown _____   **6** green _____

 **2** **Listen and number.**

 a

 b [1]

 c

3 **Read and colour. Then look and write.**

blue

red

brown

green

orange

yellow

1 I'm wearing _____**brown**_____ shoes and a _____ skirt.

2 I'm wearing a _____ T-shirt and _____ trousers.

3 I'm wearing a _____ dress and _____ socks.

 **Write. Then listen and check.**

bed   boots   jumper   ~~pyjamas~~
pyjamas   school   shoes   T-shirt

1
Take off your **pyjamas** .

2
Put on your _____ .

3
Put on your _____ .

4
It's time for _____ .

5
Take off your _____ .

6
Take off your _____ .

7
Put on your _____ .

8
It's time for _____ .

5  Listen and match. Then trace.

①

nurse

purple

bird

T-shirt

skirt

②

③

④

⑤
purple

6  Match. Then listen and say.

bird   horse   mice   train

baby   skirt   torch   bike

 **Find and colour the hats from the story. Write the number.**

_____ hats.

  **What's missing? Draw and write.**

black   dress
hat   pink

1   I'm wearing a _____ _____ .

2   I'm wearing a _____ _____ .

9  **Write. Then say.**

| chef | firefighter | ~~nurse~~ | police officer |

(1) I'm a __nurse__ .

(2) I'm a _____ .

(3) I'm a _____ .

(4) I'm a _____ .

10  **Read. Then find and number.**

a I'm wearing black trousers and black shoes. I'm wearing a hat. ☐ 4

b I'm wearing a white dress, a hat and black shoes. ☐

c I'm wearing a helmet and white boots. ☐

d I'm wearing a T-shirt and trousers. I'm wearing white shoes and a big hat. ☐

11   **Read. Then look and write.**

| boots | ~~dress~~ | hat | jumper | shoes |
| skirt | socks | trousers | T-shirt |

1

I'm wearing

a **dress** ,

a _____

and _____ .

2

I'm wearing

a _____ ,

a _____

and _____ .

3

I'm wearing

_____ ,

a _____

and _____ .

12  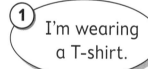 **Read and match. Then say.**

1 I'm wearing a T-shirt.

2 I'm wearing trousers.

3 I'm wearing a dress.

LOOK!

I'm wearing black boots.

Put on your shoes.

Take off your hat.

8 Weather

  Look and read. Then circle and write.

cloudy   cool   rainy   snowy   ~~sunny~~   windy

Is it rainy?
Yes / (No)
It's ___sunny___.

Is it windy?
Yes / No
It's _____.

Is it sunny?
Yes / No
It's _____.

Is it cloudy?
Yes / No
It's _____.

Is it snowy?
Yes / No
It's _____.

Is it cool?
Yes / No
It's _____.

Ask and answer. Write *Yes* or *No*.

Do you like...	Me	My friend, _____
...rainy days?		
...sunny days?		
...cloudy days?		
...snowy days?		
...windy days?		

   What do you like? Draw, write and say.

cloudy   rainy   snowy   sunny   windy

1   I like _____ days.   **2**   I don't like _____ days.

 **Look. Then read and number.**

Picture 1

Picture 2

1 It's cloudy. ☐1

2 I'm wearing a T-shirt and trousers. ☐

3 I've got a train. ☐

4 I like pizza. ☐

5 I'm wearing a dress. ☐

6 I like chicken. ☐

7 I've got a doll. ☐

8 Look at my dog. It's big. ☐

9 It's sunny. ☐

10 I'm wearing boots. ☐

5   Find and colour.

blue   boot   moose   scooter   shoe   two

6   Listen and circle the odd one out.

1

2

3

4

Listen and number. Then match.

1

   Read and draw.

9  **Look and write.**
Then listen and check.

| Saturday | Thursday | ~~Tuesday~~ | Wednesday |

Monday

_____

<u>Tuesday</u>

Friday

_____

_____

Sunday

---

10 **Read. Then look and ✓ or ✗.**

Monday	Tuesday	Wednesday	Thursday	Friday	Saturday	Sunday
☀	🌀	🌧	❄	☀	☁	☁

1 It's Tuesday. It's windy. ✓   **2** It's Saturday. It's rainy. ☐

3 It's Thursday. It's rainy. ☐   **4** It's Monday. It's snowy. ☐

5 It's Sunday. It's cloudy. ☐   **6** It's Friday. It's sunny. ☐

 **Read. Then find and write.**

I CAN DO IT!

| cloudy | snowy | sunny | ~~windy~~ |

He's in the garden.

It's ___windy___ . 3

I'm wearing big boots!

It's _____ . ☐

She's got a bike.

It's _____ . ☐

I'm wearing a jumper.

It's _____ . ☐

  Look and write.

I like (i n a r y) days.

I like _____ days.

It's (w y d i n).

It's _____ .

LOOK!

It's windy.

I like snowy days.

Do you like rainy days?

Picture dictionary

Numbers

 one two three four five six seven eight nine ten

 eleven twelve thirteen fourteen fifteen

 sixteen seventeen eighteen nineteen twenty

My toys

ball   doll   bike   boat   car   train   kite

My family

sister brother   granny grandad   aunt   uncle   cousin   friend

My body

head   arms   hands   fingers   legs   feet   toes   body

My face

| face | eyes | ears | nose | mouth | hair |

Animals

cow   horse   goat   sheep   duck   hen   turkey

Food

apple   fish   banana   pizza   chicken   rice   egg   hot dog   burger

Clothes

T-shirt   skirt   socks   shoes   trousers   dress   hat

Weather

rainy   sunny   cloudy   snowy   windy   cool

Christmas

 1 Look and write. Then say.

Christmas tree   present   ~~Santa~~   star   stocking

1

Santa _____

2

_____

3

_____

4

_____

5

_____

2 Look and colour.

1 red   **2** green   **3** black   **4** blue   **5** yellow

Valentine's Day

1 Write the words.

card ~~chocolates~~
flowers   heart

1

2

3

4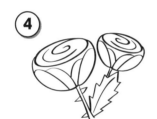

Crossword:

1. c
2. h _ _ _
3. c _ _ _
4. o
   l
   a
   t
   4. _ _ _ _ e _ _
   s

2 ✏ Draw a present for a friend.

Here's a present

for _____.

Easter

  **1** **Look and write. Then say.**

| chick   egg   flower   ~~rabbit~~ |

rabbit _____ _____ _____

 **2** **Read. Then count and write.**

1 How many chicks? 5   **2** How many flowers? ☐

3 How many eggs? ☐   **4** How many rabbits? ☐

Pearson Education Limited
Edinburgh Gate
Harlow
Essex CM20 2JE
England
and Associated Companies throughout the world.

Poptropica English

© Pearson Education Limited 2017

Editorial and project management by hyphen

All rights reserved; no part of this publication may be reproduced, stored in a retrieval system, or transmitted in any form or by any means, electronic, mechanical, photocopying, recording, or otherwise without the prior written permission of the Publishers.

First published 2017

ISBN: 978-1-292-09145-7

Set in Fiendstar 17/21pt

Illustrators: Adam Clay, Moreno Chiacchiera (Beehive Illustration), Chan Sui Fai, Tom Heard (The Bright Agency), Andrew Hennessey, Marek Jagucki, Sue King (Plum Pudding Illustration), Stephanine Lau, Yam Wai Lun, Katie McDee, Bill McGuire (Shannon Associates), Jorge Santillan (Beehive Illustration), Jackie Stafford, Olimpia Wong

All other images © Pearson Education Limited

Every effort has been made to trace the copyright holders and we apologize in advance for any unintentional omissions. We would be pleased to insert the appropriate acknowledgement in any subsequent edition of this publication.